Zayn's Wa ...

Written by Michelle C. Wordsworth

Illustrated by Charles Nnana-Kalu

ISBN 978-1-8384707-0-8

Teletypemedia

Dedication

This book is dedicated to my brothers
Devon and Mark, thanks for your support
and encouragement.

For all the boys and men in the world.

Acknowledgement

Thanks to my daughter Marina.

It's Zayn's birthday lunch.
"Is that my present?" asks Zayn.
"Yes," says Mum.
"Can I open it?
"*OK!*" says Dad.

Zayn opens his present.
"Brilliant!" shouts Zayn. "My own watch, just like you Dad. It's the best present I've ever had. Thank you."

Dad always wears a watch and knows what time it is. Zayn likes how Dad's watch looks on his wrist.

Everyday Dad teaches Zayn how to tell the time.

Zayn likes how the second hand moves around
the clock.
"Can you count in fives?" asks Dad.
"*Yes*," says Zayn. "5, 10, 15, 20, 25, 30."
"Well done."

Zayn wears his watch everyday and everywhere he goes.

"Morning Mum."
"Morning Zayn."
"Are we going to the park today?"
"Yes."
"Yay!"

In the afternoon, Mum takes Zayn and his
sister Grace to the park.
"There's Dean," says Grace.
"Dean!" shouts Zayn.

"Hi Zayn."
"Hi Dean, I got this watch for my birthday."
"It's really nice," says Dean.
"It helps me learn to tell the time."

The next day.
Zayn wakes up early for school.
"Oh No!" shouts Zayn. "Where's my watch?"
Zayn's watch isn't' on the table next to his bed.

Zayn looks inside his bed, under his bed.
No watch.
"What are you doing?" asks Mum.
"I can't find my watch."
 "Where did you put it?"
"I don't remember, it's disappeared."
"Zayn, things don't disappear."

"It's gone forever," says Zayn.
"Let's have a look downstairs," says Mum.

"I've found it!" shouts Zayn. "It's under the table."
"Finally," sighs Mum.
"What's going on in here?" asks Dad.

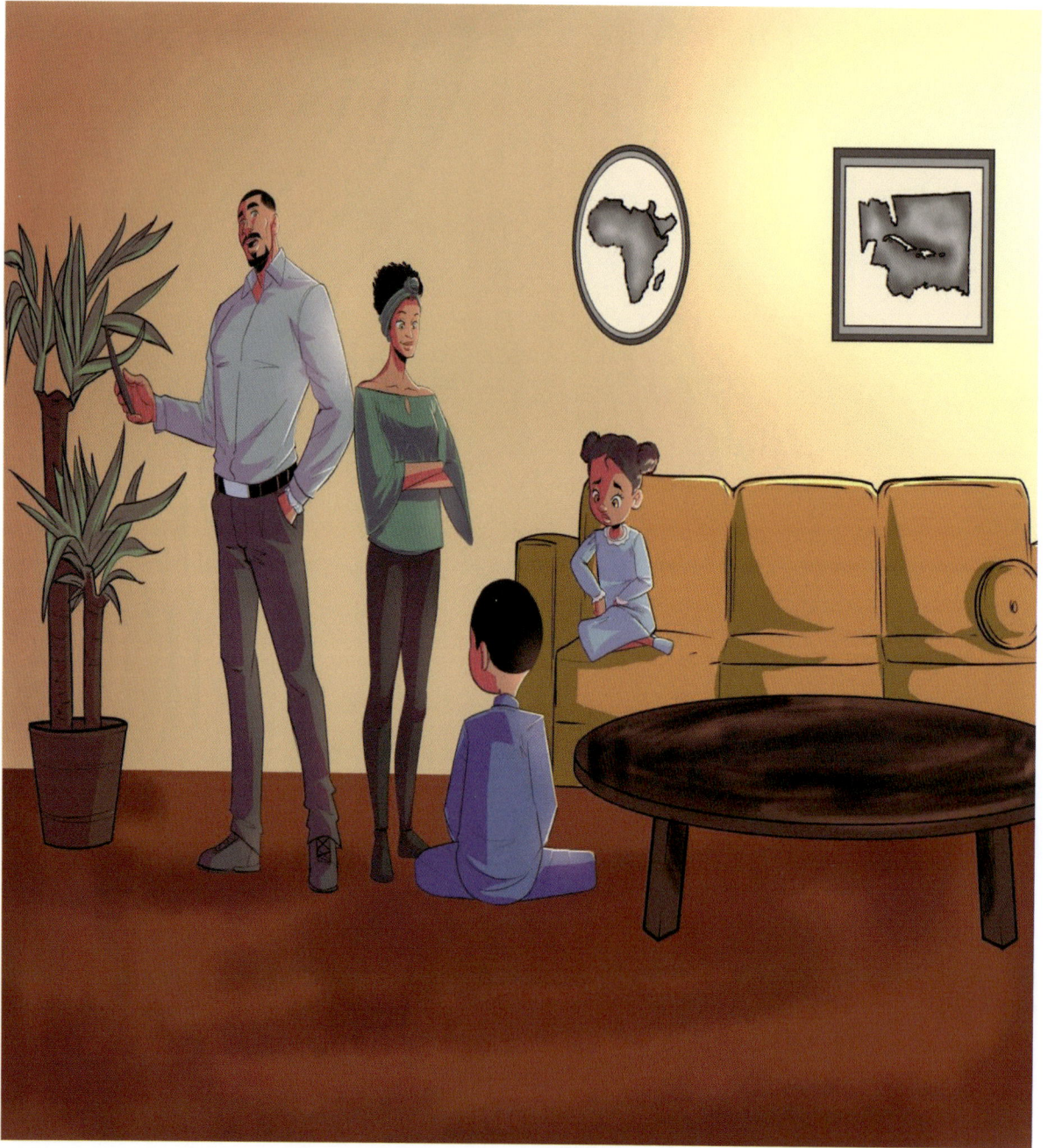

"I lost my watch."
"*WHAT!*" says Dad.
"He misplaced it," says Mum.

"Zayn."
"Yes Dad."
"It's important to look after things."
"Sorry Dad."
"Don't worry."

"I'm glad you found your watch."
"Me too."

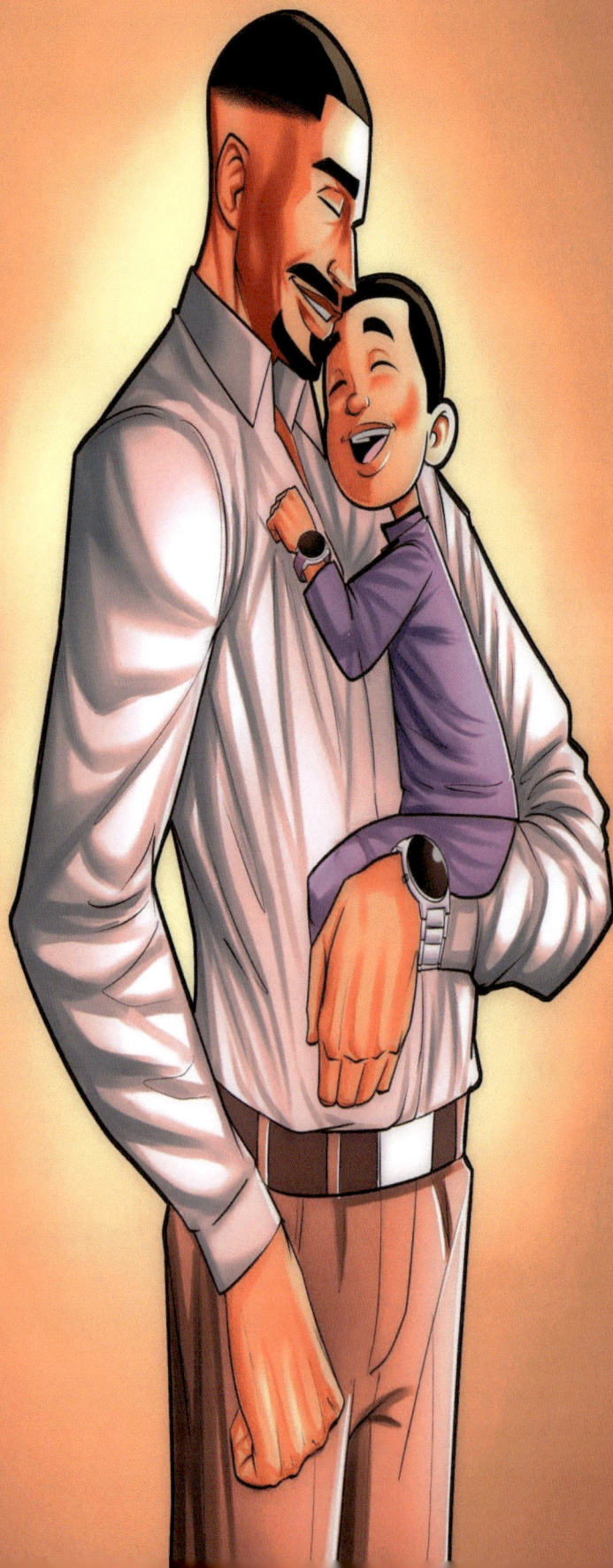

Tips for learning to tell the time

Start with analogue clock.
Make it fun!
Let's draw a clock face.
What time is bedtime?
How many seconds in a minute?
Teach them to count to 60 by fives.
Practice writing numbers.
Jump on the spot for 1 minute, watch the clock ticking.
Ask questions; Is it AM or PM?

Practice, Practice, Practice!

Clock Face

Time

60 seconds = 1 minute

60 minutes = 1 hour

24 hours = 1 day

7 days = 1 week

365 days = 1 year

Printed in Great Britain
by Amazon